HOLIDAY FUN

EARTH DAY

KIM THOMPSON

NorwoodHouse Press

Cataloging-in-Publication Data

Names: Thompson, Kim.
Title: Earth Day / Kim Thompson.
Description: Buffalo, NY : Norwood House Press, 2027. | Series: Holiday fun | Includes glossary and index.
Identifiers: ISBN 9781978580596 (pbk.) | ISBN 9781978580602 (library bound) | ISBN 9781978580619 (ebook)
Subjects: LCSH: Earth Day--Juvenile literature. | Environmentalism--Juvenile literature.
Classification: LCC GE195.5 T548 2027 | DDC 394.262--dc23

Published in 2027 by
Norwood House Press
2544 Clinton Street
Buffalo, NY 14224

Designer: Rhea Magaro
Editor: Tricia Hoffman

Photo credits: Cover, p. 1 Harinnita Detta/Shutterstock.com; p. 4 Irina Starikova1811/Shutterstock.com; p. 5 Studio Romantic/Shutterstock.com; p. 7 KawaiiS/Shutterstock.com; pp. 8, 15 New Africa/Shutterstock.com; p. 9 Library of Congress; p. 10 Sergei Bachlakov/Shutterstock.com; p. 13 DJ Creative Studio/Shutterstock.com; pp. 16, 18 PeopleImages/Shutterstock.com; p. 19 Pixel-Shot/Shutterstock.com; p. 21 narikan/Shutterstock.com;

Printed in the United States of America

CPSIA compliance information: Batch #CSNHP27: For further information contact Norwood House Press at 1-800-237-9932.

TABLE OF CONTENTS

Earth Day Is Here! 4
A Special Day 6
How to Celebrate 12
Glossary 22
Thinking Questions 23
Index 24
About the Author 24

EARTH DAY IS HERE!

Your T-shirt says THINK **GREEN**, LIVE CLEAN. You grab your work gloves. You are ready!

On this **holiday**, people do their part to make the world a little better. It is Earth Day!

A SPECIAL DAY

Earth Day comes every spring.

It is always on April 22nd.

Happy
Earth
Day!

The first Earth Day was in 1970. People held a **rally**. They were concerned about the **environment**. They let people know how important it is to take care of our planet.

COME DOWN TO EARTH
SOUVENIRS OF EARTH DAY APRIL 22nd 1970
ORGANIC
PENNSYLVANIA DUTCH COUNTRY
SOIL
THE VALLEY FARM AND ENVIRONMENTAL ACTION COALITION
HAPPY EARTH DAY!
DIG IT! BUY DIRT HERE!
THE VALLEY FARM BOOTH
FLOWER POTS
Buy a Pot 50¢ 60¢ and Plant it
ENVELOPES 25¢
Mail dirt to a friend
(stamps included)

NO MORE
PLASTIC
REFUSE
PLASTIC
Mars
CRUNCH
Reese
Butterfinger
SNICKERS

By 1990, Earth Day was celebrated around the world. Each year, more than a billion people join in.

HOW TO CELEBRATE

People form teams at work, at school, and in their communities. They decide on a project. Then, they get to work!

OLUNTEER

Some teams help the land. They pick up **litter**. They plant trees. They make homes for **pollinators**.

Some teams help the water. They test drinking water. They pick up plastic on beaches, so turtles and other animals do not eat it and get sick.

Some teams help the air. They reduce **pollution** by walking or biking instead of driving cars. They make posters about **climate change**.

On Earth Day, people work together to make a difference.

The planet gets a little greener, and everyone is happy!

GLOSSARY

climate change (KLYE-mit chaynj): global warming and other changes in weather patterns that are happening because of human activities

environment (en-VYE-ruhn-muhnt): all of nature, including the air, land, freshwater bodies, and oceans

green (green): a color used as a symbol for growing things and a healthy planet

holiday (HAH-li-day): a special day; a day when most people do not go to school or work because of a religious or national celebration

litter (LIT-ur): scraps of trash and garbage that are scattered around carelessly

pollinators (PAH-luh-nay-turz): bees, butterflies, bats, and other animals that carry pollen from plant to plant so that plants can make fruits and reproduce

pollution (puh-LOO-shuhn): harmful materials from factories and other sources that damage the air, water, and soil

rally (RAL-ee): a large meeting for a purpose

THINKING QUESTIONS

1. When is Earth Day?
2. When was the first Earth Day?
3. Where is Earth Day celebrated?
4. Who participates in Earth Day?
5. Give examples of Earth Day projects. How do they help Earth?

INDEX

air 18

climate change 18

first 8

land 14

pollution 18

teams 12, 14, 17, 18

water 17

world 5, 11

ABOUT THE AUTHOR

Kim Thompson lives in Columbus, Ohio, with her husband and two funny cats. She has written many books for kids. Her favorite ways to help Earth—on Earth Day and every day—are to plant a garden and drive her electric car. Her favorite holiday is the one that is coming up next!